Dear Parents,

Congratulations for choosing a fun and entertaining way to help your child learn to interact with others in pleasing, socially acceptable ways!

Children have the ability to be good, and they are often eager to please. However, they often don't understand their own egocentric or self-centered behavior. This self-centeredness often leads to misbehavior, and the misbehavior often leads to negative responses from others. All too soon, your child can be caught in a destructive cycle of negative action and reaction.

The purpose of the **HELP ME BE GOOD** books is to help your child break the cycle of negative action and reaction. Your child will learn how to replace misbehavior with acceptable behavior. Each **HELP ME BE GOOD** book is designed to do the following in an enjoyable way:

1. Define a misbehavior
2. Explain the cause of the misbehavior
3. Discuss the negative effects of the misbehavior
4. Offer suggestions for replacing the misbehavior with acceptable behavior

While it is effective to read the individual **HELP ME BE GOOD** books when a need arises, the series was designed to follow the normal development of young children. Consequently, presenting the books to your child in the order in which they are listed on the back cover of this book also works well.

As you and your child read the **HELP ME BE GOOD** books, your child will develop good behavior that will help build positive self-esteem and healthy relationships. Reading the books will also help to create a more friendly, happy atmosphere in your home. Thank you for allowing me to be a part of this exciting endeavor!

Sincerely,

Joy Berry

Joy Berry

Joy Berry Enterprises, Inc.
146 West 29th St., Suite 11RW
New York, NY 10001

Cover Design & Art Direction: John Bellaud
Art Production: Geoff Glisson
Printed in Mexico
ISBN 978-1-60577-129-8

A Help Me Be Good Book About

Being Mean

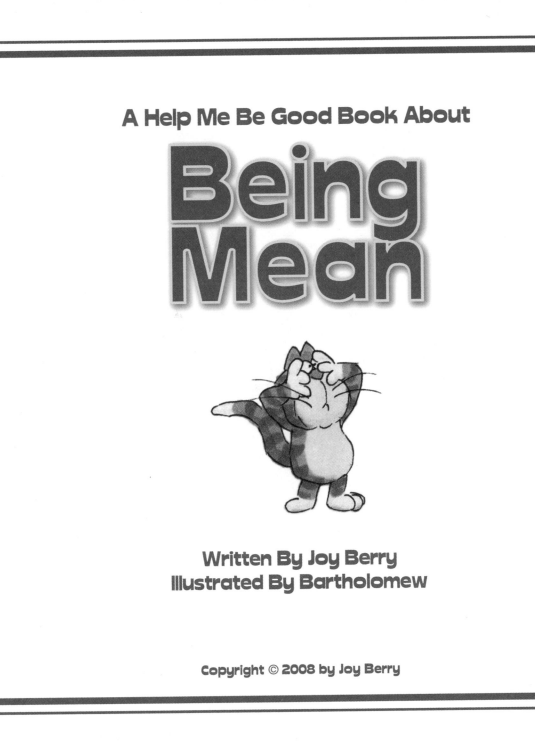

Written By Joy Berry
Illustrated By Bartholomew

This is Robbie and Katie. Reading about Robbie and Katie can help you understand why people are sometimes mean. It can also help you avoid being mean to others.

If you do something on purpose to hurt another person, you are being mean. When you are being mean to someone, you intentionally hurt the person's

- body,
- feelings, or
- belongings.

Sometimes people are mean because they want attention. They want to be noticed.

Being mean will not get you the kind of attention you want or need.

Try not to be mean when you need or want attention. Do these things instead:

- Tell someone in a kind way that you need attention.
- Ask the person to spend some time with you.

Sometimes people are mean because they don't know a better way to be funny. They want to make themselves or other people laugh.

Doing something that hurts someone or damages something is never funny. Being mean is never funny!

Try not to be mean when you want to be funny. Before you do something you think is funny to another person, be certain that

- the person will agree that what you are doing is funny,
- the person will not be hurt in any way, and
- no one's belongings will be damaged.

Some people are mean because they feel
angry or frustrated and don't know a better
way to express their anger or frustration.

Being mean is not a good way to express anger or frustration. Being mean often creates situations that will make you feel even more angry or more frustrated.

Try not to express your anger or frustration by being mean. It is OK to express your anger or frustration by crying, yelling, jumping up and down, or hitting something that cannot be damaged (such as a pillow, punching bag, or bed). To avoid bothering anyone, you might need to go outside or into a room by yourself and close the door.

Some people are mean because they have been hurt and they want to get back at someone. These people try to make themselves feel better by

- hurting the person who has hurt them or
- hurting someone else.

Getting back at someone is not a good way to make yourself feel better when you are hurt. Getting back at someone might make the person want to get back at you, and you might get hurt again.

Try not to be mean when you have been hurt. Do these things instead:

- Talk to the person who has hurt you. Let the person know that you have been hurt and that you feel bad about whatever happened.
- Stay away from the person who has hurt you until you are certain that he or she will not hurt you again.

It is important to treat other people the way you want to be treated. If you don't want other people to be mean to you, you should not be mean to them.

Visit us on the web at www.joyberryenterprises.com!